BOND WITH WOUND

RARE BUT FAKE

SUMEET KUMAR

Sumeet Kumar

Sumeet Kumar , A adult who experiences many phases of life , a well known writer and a writer of new era . In reality he is a writter as well as singer (as a hobby) and a standup comedian . Very exciting and interesting fact about him is that he is author of New era i.e. he starts his journey of writing at the age when he was going to schools to get the study .His some famous works i.e. Maturity Of Love (Genre - Love),Privacy For Dream (Genre - Middle Class), Army Squad ofLove (Genre- The Seperation of Army Love), 5 Days of Love(Genre- Temporarily Love), Th e Endearment Of Love(Genre - Historical Era Of Love), Social Destruction Indo-Pak (Genre - The Story of The Love At The Time Of Division Of India And Pakistan), Middle Class Soul (Genre - The Dreams of Middle Class), The Accursed Kanatpur (Genre -The Horrific Story Of A Village), Wrong Number (Genre -The Suspenseful Physco Killer Story), The Secrecy OfDeadly Midnight (Genre - The Suspense About a Crime),Fragile Religious Of Death (Genre- The Death Of A TrustfulPerson), Nature Vs Science (Genre - The Future Battle Between Nature And Science In A Horrific Way), Generic Man (Genre - The Dream of I.I.T), The Unconsious 12 Hours(Genre - The Illusion At Stage Of Comma), The StrangeBurden (Genre - The

Burden Of Love) , Her Existence (Genre- The Female Pain In The Society) , Jockstrap Prize (Genre -The True Story Of A National Athlete) , H Man [Hindi] (Genre - Superhero Tragic Story), H Man [English] (Genre - Superhero Tragic Story) , Maturity Of Love [Englsih] (Genre - Love) and many more are available on various geners on the offcial platform of Amazon, Flipkart and Notionpress. You can buy them from there.

Contents

Preface

Maybe the life is not perfect for me rather I work hard to improve my self in front of those who literally does,nt care about me for a single second of moment ,I never cried usually but today the frame of sadness behind me tried to forget me about what we have inside between both of us and what kind of relation we kept for both of us in the light journey of life ,In this story there was nothing to hide neither to create but there was alot of satisfaction about what we have to achieve in this world and what we not ?

Acknowledgements

Sumeet Kumar

Sumeet Kumar , A adult who experiences many phases of life , a well known writer and a writer of new era . In reality he is a writter as well as singer (as a hobby) and a standup comedian . Very exciting and interesting fact about him is that he is author of New era i.e. he starts his journey of writing at the age when he was going to schools to get the study .His some famous works i.e. Maturity Of Love (Genre - Love),Privacy For Dream (Genre - Middle Class), Army Squad ofLove (Genre- The Seperation of Army Love), 5 Days of Love(Genre- Temporarily Love), Th e Endearment Of Love(Genre - Historical Era Of Love), Social Destruction Indo-Pak (Genre - The Story of The Love At The Time Of Division Of India And Pakistan), Middle Class Soul (Genre - The Dreams of Middle Class), The Accursed Kanatpur (Genre -The Horrific Story Of A Village), Wrong Number (Genre -The Suspenseful Physco Killer Story), The Secrecy OfDeadly Midnight (Genre - The Suspense About a Crime),Fragile Religious Of Death (Genre- The Death Of A TrustfulPerson), Nature Vs Science

(Genre - The Future Battle Between Nature And Science In A Horrific Way), Generic Man (Genre - The Dream of I.I.T), The Unconsious 12 Hours(Genre - The Illusion At Stage Of Comma), The StrangeBurden (Genre - The Burden Of Love) , Her Existence (Genre- The Female Pain In The Society) , Jockstrap Prize (Genre -The True Story Of A National Athlete) , H Man [Hindi] (Genre - Superhero Tragic Story), H Man [English] (Genre - Superhero Tragic Story) , Maturity Of Love [Englsih] (Genre - Love) and many more are available on various geners on the offcial platform of Amazon, Flipkart and Notionpress. You can buy them from there.

CHAPTER ONE

BLIND DEATH

Today neither any story starts from life nor ends on it, because today there is neither a safari to reveal anything nor there is any wish to say anything which is related to my life, who wants to write, wants to say and,
To be clear, I want to enumerate, something has changed in my life in a few months, that even without wanting to, I have come close to those people from whom I had once vowed to stay away, I feel happy that myself I am moving forward after killing because I have lived my life, now he is never mine, love, friendship, family, this is his, I am alsoSomewhere I am included in them, but I never felt that they are really my own, it seems that I am lost somewhere in their fate, I have wandered from myself, in my own arms, now I do not feel like going close, Because I know that those who were mine are never my own, this life is becoming a puzzle for me, where the destination is close to us, the path is a maze, everyone's face is the same, but my hope is different from all of them, from whom I I don't know the truth of love Whatever I am, he had come with only one intention to make her mine, some of his love is missing in my every loneliness feeling that I can never make him aware of myself, every day is a new battle, I would have thought that Go ahead, create a new world of your own, but will it ever be possible to accept that even in this way, he will be seen wandering somewhere in them, every single story of mine is now asking many questions to me, from morning to night till dark she's been something to me,

Is this life really my own, I have taken it from someone else, it is said that when people change, their nature also changes, I saw myself changing but my nature is still the same, I don't know why I am not wrong because I have fulfilled the promises I made to him, but I am not able to fulfill the promises I made to myself and I don't know why Ash has remained, I can't even say why that has become , Now the one who is on
journey in between from himself that he should return,I should go and

change myself, I am not weak, I know this much, because if I am weak, then the world can never live for so long, I have broken every wall which is guaranteed by my nafs, I I have strangled myself, I have killed myself for one person, this is for his community, this story is not related to love, this is my story, my only identity, which I can neither erase now nor from myself I can overcome, don't know the specialty of the day but today,It is necessary that the curtain should be removed from some secret because now is not the time to stop myself, to make myself safe, this life will take something away today, by giving it something, but whatever happens in my life, I say this in return , I wish that if only for once, but my nature should be only mine, be loyal to me and not for anyone else.

Childhood memories are also nothing special because life at that time was also related to the same atmosphere and gatherings as I am today.Loves me too, I have nothing to do with life, nothing is inferior, what are the moments that I have seen in my account, the same moments are making each and every nature of my future the identity of my past today, of such a past We are creating identity in which we do not want to see, why we often recommend the same thing which we never have our own power, why no other person like Shravan was born in this world.Why Radha and Krishna's love was not repeated again, why Ram and Sita didn't become each other? Why is the tradition of the world still there?

CHAPTER TWO

THE LOST CHILD

Why do I consider myself alone when I have that owner, my own incomplete dreams, my own incomplete memories and the desire not to see that journey, nowadays I laugh at myself that I have changed so much that in coming own gross,I have become hated, these are not my words but I know the right about me, this is the tyranny of the society, whose safari now seems false, no one seems to be his own, that means this world was there earlier also, it was on the public thinking that it was safe for them. maybe , I am wrong person myself, this world is not as soft and innocent as it looks from outside, its every move is a poison, life does not grow after living, my condition has deteriorated. This is the public that I am,I think that I can never do it and even if I am capable, then it does not become my fate, I wish this world was like a dream, which is included in the nature of the night, but as soon as the morning comes, every glimpse of its light disappears.

if I Some people are hated, so why am I in their intentions? Why don't I go away, and why do I remember them when they are not my own? The desire to show off has increased so much that I can neither keep them away from me nor bring them close to me, on one side there is no waste in my part, I know it is on two sides and both of them are in my part. Yes, is he himself responsible for this, this society, some of its people? Who is responsible? this is me myself there are so many questions that when Even if I go out to find the answer, the whole evening will pass and at night I will see only the shell of an egg.

songs album like, Life has become ordinary like sometimes happiness sometimes sorrow, and I don't even know how to deal with it, on one side is my Fatute Wali ringtone and on the other side is my memories and some people are also included in this Whom my soul wants to forget but the heart is useless because its nature seems to change every night, and it,I don't know where the control bell is, and how would I know because it is on the other side of life, from there I remembered that there are some memories these days which are not my own, and may never be mine even after being mine. Now a days some relations visit, even if I don't want to see their gross, I would see them four times a day, are they my compulsions, this is my condition, I am imprisoned in my place, I want to free myself, but how I don't even know if I should do this...

CHAPTER THREE

JUST THROW AND LET SEE

The journey is so long that it doesn't go anywhere, what I want to write never stops in its realization, Life becomes a comedy when you are capable of something but you don't have it even though you are capable of it, means what is going on Friends, sometimes society does not come in life, people who are happy with you are not necessarily yours, it means that who is in the world and whose brother is all money's chunker, what I had said earlier that my life is a song album

there was no one in this world for you except the trap of money against the relationship, what I said earlier that my whole life is an album of songs, and the most favorite wali jo meri line in it is that "JUST THROW THE MONEY AND LET SEE THE SHOW " yeah its my life So it's just like that because all the people I have met have turned out to be like this only talk of money from day till night sometimes Ayesha feels that I myself am a pimp because everyday I am doing the same , I am giving my thing to everyone after weighing it.

Some words of wisdom that I want to tell everyone like a lesson, who is like me, if you want to take forward every single story of your life, then stop meeting others, stop paying attention to other's words, the world is weak to you. Compromise is also right, but never consider yourself wrong and wise, because life is not going to give you a chance to live again, and even if you give it by mistake, is it necessary that your condition should improve from before, this can also happen. how are you Even worse, and if it is correct, then live your life, such a shadow where in times of danger, your relationships will come in the form of low validity of a bank balance.......

Well, now I want to tell the secret to myself, which are my own as well as strangers, because the relationships that I have made, these have become my destiny for me, they are mine as well as strangers, what to tell is a long There is a story in which the way is somewhere,And the destination is like a mirage, such a mirage which shows dreams but never supports to fulfill them.

SOURCE OF EXISTENCE

"

YOU
ARE THE SOURCE
OF MY
EVERY WISH
NO MATTER
WHERE
I LIVE
MY OUTLOOK LIFE IS
ALWAYS
DEPEND ON
YOU .

"

THE WORST MEMORIES

Today again I am going to make a new beginning from the same path, the destination for which death was not possible for me, Ishq Ruh tried a lot to be careful, but it seems

Life has no special control over its intensity, I want to leave the journey of God and recite a new journey, but the matter of insult is that my place,Till date, I have not seen any clear benefit from him, even life wants me to respect myself as God that one day I can go away from myself.

This life doesn't seem perfect, no matter how much I run away, I still bump into myself somewhere, I think that at times,True, try to fulfill your every wish by yourself, but now it does not happen and I do not even know why it does not happen, now I am

It has become a habit of the day which makes me weak in myself. Every day my story is not different from the rest but my words are definitely different from the rest.

I never thought in my life that I would do it, but if my circumstances change, my nature will also change in the same way, my

Am I not myself the reason for the anger? How do I tell people who are walking away from me because of this, I don't want to change myself

If I don't change then maybe some people will change me, I have made up my mind to go away from everyone who is with me

Hash baat whatever I am saying because because of my going back neither their life is going to change nor mine, but yes point of peace was already in my assembly Will definitely give me peace that he will be happy even without me, his party and maybe will be more?

   what kind of memories of childhood which is nothing special but whenever I think about them, Ayesha feels that there was a peace in her memories of that past.

Where it was not a disaster of running away from myself, from school life

to home life was absolutely normal, always thinks this in childhood
I was wondering when will I grow up, and when I have grown up, that thinks what friend? Why did you have to grow up?

The life of that time was like a dynamite, that too of happiness, but today's life is just a circle, that too of sorrows
Will find because it has every single story of God's grace.

By the way, it has been forgotten in my circle that I also have a story which is Gujarati through my city, through my locality and of that locality. Name? Tell me what should be?
Well, I know that you all do not know that I belong to which locality? Some or the other person makes mistake and I am talking about the same mistake. Huh? Didn't understand the meaning, I am also trying to understand my life very closely, but till today I could not understand what happened
Is? what is this life Well God, the beginning of life means I have started from Bihar, means I am a resident of Gaya, means Gaya in the name of the place itself, how can someone come in his life, it is just a matter of thinking? And the identity of my name is also something like this, Soch Ram Singh.

So let me tell you all about myself, if the time is long then it is because I have been well since then, it is not that I am bad in studies, I got good marks in 10th class but when in 12th class If I didn't do that, would you have come well at that time also?
A state in Eastern India

Gaya Jaunpur.....

The story of Vaishé cast is very unique where people have gone so far in their life that too with a good thought, there are still some people who come with a thought which is absolutely not necessary for the society and neither for us. For the future ahead because we know we need a new save of someone's thinking and hard work to move forward.

Well, if I start telling the things of the society, then my story will remain incomplete, but I can't even separate God from himself.
Sumit Tripathi, this is the identity of my name due to which everyone knows me, that too not because of me, because of my sister-in-law, that means because of our father, now you all must have read that,s why i just think there was little coversation start with another language which we called english , We have used it, our brother-in-law is that person, who asks for his hard work and his passion, he is always the same.

It is said that "If you don't make hard work, then you will eat roti in the house", they always say this, but till today nothing has been understood about their words, people speak only Maghai, but they speak and do many other things with it. There are also, now what do we tell about those who do and speak. The more educated people are in this locality, the more we feel that no one is well educated, see the rest of the people, don't feel bad because something is like this, every year lakhs Engineers pass and roam around bash with degrees, some people say that they are out there, some people say that they get employment, but even if they do, you tell me, one is our government which does not give them job and one is their family members who are there all the time. It is said to earn money, this life is very different if we see the life of other cities, it is not necessary that the situation should be like this everywhere.

I am also brought up among them and there is something like this in our luck, we have enjoyed life in a green way but have never enjoyed unemployment, now it will be difficult to bear it for a few days because we got I have completed my graduation and that too from Magadh University, but I never dreamed of completing my graduation, my father-in-law put so much pressure on us to do what we didn't want to do even after telling us, this is the way of life. Because har baad mein jeet hai, these songs bhi aaj gajab ki maya paal dete and we feel they are relatable to our life very much, ayesha kabhi matt sochiye they relatable to us.
There is no part of love and affection which you told but we used to love a girl so much that we fought with all our might for her, what was after that? After I came to know about this of Bauji, we have not forgotten the beating that he had to beat us with the belt, but we have definitely forgotten love, the name of our incomplete love was just a hope that we cannot even say anything. About him, bhale aish naam kaun rahta hai yaar 'phool kumari'.

CHAPTER SIX

PHOOL KUMARI MY LOVE

When we met Phool Kumari, when we were not children, we had grown up and used to study together at the same place, that means today's love story would have been through coaching, it would have been through school, and if it was completed at the end, it would have gone to Mandap or not. If this happens, we will be fixed with someone else, we were so attached to Phool Kumari that we fought with the entire Tola for her, then after that our Tola beat me up, but when our sister-in-law came to know about this, she did not we completely We were about to run away leaving the dog's house that we thought it was very cold anyway, if it gets cold then we will neither stay at home nor at the ghat Still the memories of Phool Kumari were haunting us, because till date we had not seen tears in her eyes, only a few days after that we got the news that her marriage was fixed, and there was no one else to get it fixed. It was our brother-in-law, Because both Bauji and Shukla were langothiya yaar, wait you are telling everyone about Shukla ji also.

Shukla ji is that person who, if our brother-in-law is Sura, then he is moon, if it is day, then that night is such a pair, but both of them are proud in their profession. that trade lovers, means you all in a different line
Don't take their profession, what I mean to say is that they get married, and got it done in our flower girl's marriage itself, when we heard this, we were very angry at first, we thought that we We would have done it, but when we remembered Bauji's death, we thought that if we do not do anything then it is okay, otherwise we will not be beaten by him again, then what was there, he got married and that too in front of our eyes. we even ate his wedding dinner
That too, there were whole vegetables and cottage cheese, two black berries and one white berries were also present in the food;
After all, our body had already given us freedom, after that day our only love also gave us back the same freedom and we left that city and came to

another city with only her memories.

CHAPTER SEVEN

ANGRY WITH LORD

We were very angry with Bauji because he not only separated our flower girl from us, but instead took China from us and that too in full.

For the rest of my life I thought that I would do something, then I thought of my mother and I went back from such a journey where my frog was waiting for me.I was not interested in going anywhere after that, I used to want to roam around the world Ishqiye used to demand from Bauji all the time that Hunki should get a bike.

, But there was a problem in him also, he used to say that we should get a job first, then we will know that we will take one or two wheels, life in a lot of thought.

Was walking, after the departure of Phool Kumari, there were no words of sorrow;

There was no such thing, every day we used to go ahead by convincing ourselves, but we could not get ahead in the right way, because we thought that now our

Will focus on life and do something big, and we used to go from street to neighborhood and talk to Poster till we used that money to buy a bike.

But this charity was also troubling us that if Bauji came to know that Tripathi family's poster boy is earning less money, then he

So we would have burnt him alive, but that was not going to happen because I knew that no matter how harsh she may be for us from outside, but inside,He will remain our brother-in-law, we talked about the posters for a long time but were happily thinking that why are we doing that ? That was not the case That work was small for us, because hard work, how can we lie to our father-in-law about something so small?

I was feeling very upset from inside, I could not understand what to do?

CHAPTER EIGHT

MORTAL STUDY ABOUT LIFE

After all, we talked about posters for a few months and in the locality where we talked about posters for the last time, that day some of our acquaintances What can we tell about the ruckus that happened after the relationship saw us?

The day Bauji came to know about this, on the same day he brought our favorite bike in front of us and said that you need something too.

Tell me now your father is alive and I have sent you only to study, I have never separated you from myself and getting you a bike is enough for me. It's a simple thing......

enough said this and went straight, neither did he ask about our condition nor did he stay with us for some time, I knew that Bauji was in trouble. But if we think about them at that time, then our happiness may go away from us for a while, later we come to know that the happiness we We got that too, our Bauji has given it to us.

After a few days mother called and wanted to ask us this, and informed that Phool Kumari's husband had been diagnosed a few days back and that too When I heard this from a truck, my heart was full of emotion, meaning we never thought that anything would happen to that , but when I told us,Told that he was also driving his car very fast and drunk, then when we understood the whole thing, why didn't we want to give the bike to Bauji? We understood this thing also only when Ma would tell us these things, we were scared that day and to think that whatever we had done was wrong. One more day our Gaya friend told that your brother-in-law ever broke this relationship, there were some faults in his latch.

You told him to stay and you also had bile, that day there were no tears in our eyes, but that, under the power of human, hugged ,Kiss , every queen's talk was this, we had someone and cried holding her. after that day we returned I tried in that city, but my heart had already made up my mind that now nothing remains in front of Bauji.

Jakar can't even say that I'm sorry, Bauji, I made a mistake, because she didn't have the courage, the things she told us in an old joke that she will be known in some time, that thing has now become true, she cursed herself that day. tell what?

I wanted to kill myself too because we are also a remover, even though we don't want to kill, but the shape we gave to him is not wrong, my mind was not working, our body wanted to go somewhere far away. Go away, can't even meet Phool Kumari because our relationship was different Ish Bar, we told her once that wherever you go, we will be with you no matter what the situation is, but now how can I tell her that you Can I come to you, the things of the world

Earlier we have already given many things which are wrong, if we tell this thing to him then we will be removed from his happiness. One will be his, and the other will be of our family members.

CHAPTER NINE

TROUBLING

The memory of all these was troubling me so much that in the city where we live, we have decided that we will not return to our home for the rest of our life and we will give up everything for the rest of our life, but there is little hope in life that we We think that he should go there, because life is also a puzzle, isn't it? After that day, we tried to return to that city. The heart had already accepted that there was nothing left, and did not even say this in front of Bauji sorry bauji mistake Yes, because we don't have that much courage, the things that we said jokingly in the past that it will be known in some time, that thing has now become true, what should I tell myself that day?

I wanted to kill myself too because we are also a remover, even though we don't want to kill, but the shape we gave to him is not wrong, my mind was not working, our body wanted to go somewhere far away. Go away, can't even meet Phool Kumari because our relationship was different Ish Bar, we told her once that wherever you go, we are yours.
We will be together no matter what the situation is, but now how can I tell him that can I come to you, I have already given many things about the world which is wrong, if we tell this to him, then we will remove it. Will become his happiness. Well, I am trying to return, but I cannot leave even after saying this, because this time one life, two lives will be ruined, one for him and the other for our family members.

CHAPTER TEN

INTENSITY OF PUZZLE

The memory of all these was troubling me so much that in the city where we live, we have decided that we will not return to our home for the rest of our life and we will give up everything for the rest of our life, but there is little hope in life that we They think that they should go, because life is also a puzzle, isn't it?

Fake Adore Of Family

"PERHAPS
MY RELATIONS
ARE NOT
MINE ,IF THEY
WERE THERE
WE WOULD
HAVE
BEEN TOGETHER
ONLY
IN THE
DESIRE
OF SORROWS."

For Graveyard Peace

www.ingramcontent.com/pod-product-compliance
Lightning Source LLC
Chambersburg PA
CBHW050819160726

48004CB00002B/914